science for a changing world

Prepared in cooperation with Hinsdale County, Colorado

Postwildfire Debris-Flow Hazard Assessment of the Area Burned by the 2013 West Fork Fire Complex, Southwestern Colorado

By Kristine L. Verdin, Jean A. Dupree, and Michael R. Stevens

Open-File Report 2013–1259

U.S. Department of the Interior
U.S. Geological Survey

U.S. Department of the Interior
SALLY JEWELL, Secretary

U.S. Geological Survey
SUZETTE M. KIMBALL, Acting Director

U.S. Geological Survey, Reston, Virginia: 2013

For product and ordering information:
World Wide Web: http://www.usgs.gov/pubprod
Telephone: 1-888-ASK-USGS

For more information on the USGS—the Federal source for science about the Earth,
its natural and living resources, natural hazards, and the environment:
World Wide Web: http://www.usgs.gov
Telephone: 1-888-ASK-USGS

Suggested citation:
Verdin, K.L., Dupree, J.A, and Stevens, M.R., Postwildfire debris-flow hazard assessment of the area burned by
the 2013 West Fork Fire Complex, southwestern Colorado: U.S. Geological Survey Open-File Report 2013–1259,
30 p., 3 plates, http://pubs.usgs.gov/of/2013/1259.

Cover photograph: Hope Creek, looking upstream, about 0.40 kilometers upstream from forest road
crossing. (photograph by Michael Stevens, U.S. Geological Survey, September 2013)

Contents

Figures

Table

Plates

Conversion Factors

SI to Inch/Pound

Multiply	By	To obtain
Length		
millimeter (mm)	0.03937	inch (in.)
meter (m)	3.281	foot (ft)
meter (m)	1.094	yard (yd)
kilometer (km)	0.6214	mile (mi)
Area		
square meter (m^2)	0.0002471	acre
square kilometer (km^2)	0.3861	square mile (mi^2)
Volume		
cubic meter (m^3)	35.31	cubic foot (ft^3)
cubic meter (m^3)	1.308	cubic yard (yd^3)
cubic meter (m^3)	0.0008107	acre-foot (acre-ft)
Flow rate		
millimeter per year (mm/yr)	0.03937	inch per year (in/yr)

Vertical coordinate information is referenced to the North American Vertical Datum of 1988 (NAVD 88).
Horizontal coordinate information is referenced to the North American Datum of 1983 (NAD 83).

Postwildfire Debris-Flow Hazard Assessment of the Area Burned by the 2013 West Fork Fire Complex, Southwestern Colorado

By Kristine L. Verdin, Jean A. Dupree, and Michael R. Stevens

Abstract

This report presents a preliminary emergency assessment of the debris-flow hazards from drainage basins burned by the 2013 West Fork Fire Complex near South Fork in southwestern Colorado. Empirical models derived from statistical evaluation of data collected from recently burned basins throughout the intermountain western United States were used to estimate the probability of debris-flow occurrence, potential volume of debris flows, and the combined debris-flow hazard ranking along the drainage network within and just downstream from the burned area, and to estimate the same for 54 drainage basins of interest within the perimeter of the burned area. Input data for the debris-flow models included topographic variables, soil characteristics, burn severity, and rainfall totals and intensities for a (1) 2-year-recurrence, 1-hour-duration rainfall, referred to as a 2-year storm; (2) 10-year-recurrence, 1-hour-duration rainfall, referred to as a 10-year storm; and (3) 25-year-recurrence, 1-hour-duration rainfall, referred to as a 25-year storm.

Estimated debris-flow probabilities at the pour points of the 54 drainage basins of interest ranged from less than 1 to 65 percent in response to the 2-year storm; from 1 to 77 percent in response to the 10-year storm; and from 1 to 83 percent in response to the 25-year storm. Twelve of the 54 drainage basins of interest have a 30-percent probability or greater of producing a debris flow in response to the 25-year storm. Estimated debris-flow volumes for all rainfalls modeled range from a low of 2,400 cubic meters to a high of greater than 100,000 cubic meters. Estimated debris-flow volumes increase with basin size and distance along the drainage network, but some smaller drainages also were predicted to produce substantial debris flows. One of the 54 drainage basins of interest had the highest combined hazard ranking, while 9 other basins had the second highest combined hazard ranking. Of these 10 basins with the 2 highest combined hazard rankings, 7 basins had predicted debris-flow volumes exceeding 100,000 cubic meters, while 3 had predicted probabilities of debris flows exceeding 60 percent. The 10 basins with high combined hazard ranking include 3 tributaries in the headwaters of Trout Creek, four tributaries to the West Fork San Juan River, Hope Creek draining toward a county road on the eastern edge of the burn, Lake Fork draining to U.S. Highway 160, and Leopard Creek on the northern edge of the burn. The probabilities and volumes for the modeled storms indicate a potential for debris-flow impacts on structures, reservoirs, roads, bridges, and culverts located within and immediately downstream from the burned area. U.S. Highway 160, on the eastern edge of the burn area, also is susceptible to impacts from debris flows.

Introduction

The West Fork Fire Complex consisted of three lightning-caused wildfires (the West Fork, Windy Pass, and Papoose), which burned in the San Juan and Rio Grande National Forests and private property in June and July 2013. The West Fork Fire Complex covered approximately 438 square kilometers (km^2) (107,776 acres) of land near South Fork in southwestern Colorado (Colo.) and was situated at the headwaters and along the drainage basin of the main stem of the Rio Grande and many of its tributaries. Burn severity was moderate or high for 59 percent of the area within the burn perimeter (fig. 1). The area burned is at risk of postwildfire erosion, such as that caused by debris flows and flash floods.

Debris flows have been documented after many fires in the western United States (Cannon and others, 2010) and can threaten lives, property, infrastructure, aquatic habitats, and water supplies. Wildfires can denude hillslopes of vegetation and change soil properties that affect watershed hydrology and sediment-transport processes. Even small postwildfire rainstorms can increase overland runoff that erodes soil, rock, ash, and vegetative debris from hillslopes (Cannon and others, 2008). This increased runoff concentrates in stream channels and entrains sediment that can lead to the generation of destructive debris flows. Debris-flow hazards are most significant in the 3 years (yr) following wildfires (Susan Cannon, U.S. Geological Survey, written commun., 2010).

The purpose of this report, prepared in cooperation with Hinsdale County, Colorado, is to present a preliminary emergency assessment of the debris-flow hazards from basins burned by the 2013 West Fork Fire Complex. Estimates of the predicted probability of debris-flow occurrence and volume of debris along the drainage network throughout the entire area are provided, as well as estimates for drainage basins above 54 selected basin outlets in response to 3 design storms: (1) 2-year-recurrence, 1-hour duration rainfall, referred to as a 2-year storm (a 50-percent chance of occurrence in any given year); (2) 10-year-recurrence, 1-hour-duration rainfall, referred to as a 10-year storm (a 10-percent chance of occurrence in any given year); and (3) 25-year-recurrence, 1-hour-duration rainfall, referred to as a 25-year storm (a 4-percent chance of occurrence in any given year).

Methods Used To Estimate Debris-Flow Hazards

A set of empirical equations (models) documented in Cannon and others (2010) and derived from statistical evaluation of data collected from recently burned basins throughout the intermountain western United States were used to estimate the probability of debris-flow occurrence and volumes of debris flows along the drainage network and for 54 selected drainage basins of interest. The regression equation of debris-flow probability (eq. 1) is as follows:

$$P = e^x / (1 + e^x), \tag{1}$$

where

P is the probability of debris-flow occurrence in fractional form, and

e^x is the exponential function where e represents the mathematical constant 2.718.

Equation 2 is used to calculate x:

$$x = -0.7 + 0.03(\%SG30) - 1.6(R) + 0.06(\%AB) \\ + 0.07(I) + 0.2(\%C) - 0.4(LL), \tag{2}$$

where

$\%SG30$ is the percentage of the drainage-basin area with slope equal to or greater than 30 percent;

R is drainage-basin ruggedness: the change in drainage-basin elevation (meters) divided by the square root of the drainage-basin area (square meters) (Melton, 1965);

%AB is the percentage of drainage-basin area burned at moderate to high severity;

I is average storm intensity (calculated by dividing total storm rainfall [Perica and others, 2013] by the storm duration, in millimeters per hour);

%C is clay content of the soil (percent); and

LL is the liquid limit of the soil (percentage of soil moisture by weight), which is the water content at which a soil changes from plastic to liquid behavior (Das, 1983).

Cannon and others (2010) also developed an empirical model that can be used to estimate the volume of debris flow that would likely be produced from recently burned drainage basins:

$$\text{Ln } (V) = 7.2 + 0.6(\text{Ln } SG30) + 0.7(AB)^{0.5} + 0.2(T)^{0.5} + 0.3, \tag{3}$$

where

V is the debris-flow volume, including water, sediment, and debris (cubic meters);

SG30 is the area of a drainage basin with slopes equal to or greater than 30 percent (square kilometers);

AB is the drainage-basin area burned at moderate to high severity (square kilometers);

T is the total storm rainfall (millimeters); and

0.3 is a bias-correction factor that changes the predicted estimate from a median to a mean value (Helsel and Hirsch, 2002).

Values for both probability and volume were obtained along drainage networks using the continuous parameterization technique (Verdin and Greenlee, 2003; Verdin and Worstell, 2008). With this technique, estimates of debris-flow probability and volume (Cannon and others, 2010) were obtained for every 10-meter (m) pixel along the drainage network (plates 1 and 2) as a function of conditions in the drainage basin at elevations higher than each 10-m pixel. The technique used here allows for a synoptic view of conditions throughout the entire study area, which can be used to identify specific 10-m cells or stream reaches that might be vulnerable to debris flows; the technique also aids in locating sites for installation of precipitation and streamgages and in identifying potential erosion-mitigation sites.

The base layer upon which the continuous-parameterization layers are built is the 1/3-arc-second National Elevation Dataset (Gesch and others, 2002). This digital elevation model (DEM) was projected into a Colorado-appropriate projection system (UTM, Zone 13) and processed using standard DEM-conditioning tools in ArcGIS (ESRI, 2009). Once the overland flow structure was derived using the DEM (in the form of a flow-direction matrix), the independent variables driving the probability and volume equations were evaluated for every grid cell within the extent of the DEM using the continuous-parameterization approach.

The independent variables necessary for evaluation of the probability and volume equations are of four types:

1. Topographic variables: The slope variables (%SG30, eq. 2 and SG30, eq. 3) along with the ruggedness (R, eq. 2) were all derived from the 1/3-arc-second DEM (Gesch and others, 2002) using standard geographic information system (GIS) processing techniques;

2. Soil variables: Two soil variables are used in the probability equation (eqs. 1 and 2). Both the percent clay and liquid limit of the soil were taken from the State Soil Geographic (STATSGO) database (National Soil Survey Center, 1991);

3. Burned area variables: The final burn severity dataset was obtained in the form of a shapefile from the Rio Grande Watershed Emergency Action Coordination team (RWEACT). Polygons within this dataset with a CLASS attribute of "High Burned" or "Moderate Burned" were selected to produce the mask of areas burned at moderate to high severity. This mask was used to create the required burn variables (%AB, eq. 2 and AB, eq 3);

4. Precipitation variables: Three storm events were modeled: (a) 2-year-recurrence, 1-hour duration rainfall, referred to as a 2-year storm (a 50-percent chance of occurrence in any given year); (b) 10-year-recurrence, 1-hour-duration rainfall, referred to as a 10-year storm (a 10-percent chance of occurrence in any given year); and (c) 25-year-recurrence, 1-hour-duration rainfall, referred to as a 25-year storm (a 4-percent chance of occurrence in any given year). These design events were defined using NOAA Atlas 14 (Perica and others, 2013) and its associated Precipitation Frequency (PF) Data Server. The PF Data Server allows users to download the spatially varying precipitation frequency estimates for entire states. Using these digital data allows the design storms to vary spatially, reflecting the orographic effects of the mountainous terrain and the natural variation in precipitation across the large burn area. The extremes of the design storms are (1) 2-year storm precipitation ranging from 14 to 24 millimeters (mm) across the burn area with an average precipitation of 19 mm; (2) 10-year storm ranging from 21 to 34 mm across the burn area with an average precipitation of 29 mm; and (3) 25-year storm ranging from 27 to 45 mm across the burn area with an average precipitation of 35 mm. The higher precipitation values correspond to orographic highs with the lower precipitation values occurring along the Rio Grande valley.

Once the surfaces of the independent variables were developed, the probability and volume equations were solved using map algebra for each grid cell along the drainage network, thus deriving the probability and volume surfaces.

Debris-flow hazards along a stream channel and at the pour point of a selected basin also can be represented by a combined relative debris-flow hazard ranking that is based on a combination of both probability of occurrence and volume (Cannon and others, 2010). For this assessment, the estimated values of debris-flow probability and volume were categorized into five ranked classes (following the class break-out shown on plates 1 and 2), and these class ranks were averaged to calculate the combined probability and volume relative hazard ranking (plate 3). This combined hazard ranking identifies a possible range of response from drainage basins considering both the probability of occurrence of a debris flow and the predicted volume should a debris flow occur (Cannon and others, 2010). For example, the most hazardous drainage basins will have both the highest probabilities of occurrence and the largest estimated volumes of material. Slightly less hazardous would be drainage basins modeled with a combination of either low probabilities and larger volume estimates or high probabilities and smaller volume estimates. Since five ranked classes were used, the maximum possible combined hazard ranking is 5. This would occur if both the probability and volume values fell into the highest category (probability in excess of 60 percent and volume in excess of 100,000 cubic meters [m^3]) or one of the probability and volume were in the maximum category and the other was in the second to the highest category (for an averaged value of 4.5, which is rounded to 5 for this report).

Following calculation of debris-flow probabilities, volumes, and combined relative debris-flow hazard rankings continuously along the drainage networks, the 54 basins of interest were delineated and numbered to aid in discussion of model results. These delineated drainage basins were selected to meet two criteria which were used in the original development of the probability and volume equations: (1) the size of the contributing area and (2) the size of the area burned at moderate to high severity upstream from the pour point was within the range of the data used in the development of the probability and volumes equations (0.01 to ≈30 square kilometer (km^2) for contributing area and 0.01 to ≈15 km^2 for moderate/high burned area) (Joe Gartner, U.S. Geological Survey, written commun., 2013). Debris-flow probabilities and volumes were extracted from the probability and volume surface for these locations and combined hazard rankings developed. These values are shown in plates 1, 2, and 3 and are summarized in table 1. Probability, volume, or combined hazard ranking for the numbered drainage basins represents the value at the basin outlet. Probability or hazard ranking may be higher or lower and volume rankings may be smaller for subbasins or points within the delineated drainage basins, as indicated by the stream segment analysis within the drainage basins.

Probability, Volume, and Combined Hazard Ranking of Potential Debris Flows

In response to the 2-year storm, one basin affected by the burn (basin 46; plate 1, table 1) was identified as having a probability of debris-flow occurrence greater than or equal to 60 percent, and an additional three basins (19, 21, and 47) had probabilities between 30 and 45 percent. All four of these basins are small, ranging in size from 0.3 km^2 to 1.9 km^2. Estimated volumes of debris flows for these four basins ranged from 2,400 to 12,000 cubic meters (m^3). One of these basins (46), a tributary to West Fork San Juan River, has a combined hazard ranking of 4 (the second highest modeled hazard ranking) while the remaining basins (19, 21, and 47) have combined hazard rankings of 2 or 3.

The 10-year storm resulted in the same basin (46; plate 1, table 1) with a probability of debris flow in excess of 60 percent, corresponding volume estimate of 11,000 m3, and combined hazard ranking of 4. Seven additional basins (16, 19, 21, 34, 39, 47, and 53) had probabilities of debris flow between 30 and 59 percent. These seven basins were modeled as producing volumes from 2,900 to greater than 100,000 m3. Two of these eight basins (Decker Creek [39] and a tributary to the West Fork San Juan River [46]) had combined hazard rankings of 4 while the other five basins had a combined hazard ranking of 3.

The 25-year storm shows additional basins with higher probabilities of debris flows than would result from the 2-year and 10-year storms (plate 1, table 1). Higher debris-flow volumes also are likely to be produced in response to this storm. Four basins (two tributaries to Trout Creek [19 and 21] and two tributaries to West Fork San Juan [46 and 47]) show a probability of debris flow in excess of 60 percent. An additional 8 basins (7, 15, 16, 32, 34, 39, 41, and 53) have probabilities between 30 and 59 percent. These 8 basins were modeled as producing volumes from 8,700 to greater than 100,000 m^3. For the 25-year storm, only 10 out of the 54 basins of interest are modeled as expected to produce debris-flow volumes less than about 10,000 m^3. One basin (Decker Creek [39]) is modeled as having the maximum combined hazard ranking of 5. This basin has a modeled probability of 45 percent and an expected volume greater than 100,000 m^3. An additional nine basins (17, 18, 19, 33, 41, 44, 46, 47, and 48) are modeled as having a combined hazard ranking of 4. These nine basins have probabilities from 16 to 83 percent in response to the 25-year storm and corresponding volumes from 12,000 m^3 to greater than 100,000 m^3. Six of these nine basins (17, 18, 33, 41, 44, and 48) had modeled volumes in excess of 100,000 m^3.

The only basin with a combined hazard ranking of 5 is Decker Creek (39), which drains to the eastern edge of the burn and contributes flow to a small reservoir on the eastern edge of the burn. This basin, with a modeled probability in response to the 25-year storm of 45 percent and a modeled volume of greater than 100,000 m^3 could contribute large volumes of material to the small reservoir in the event of a debris flow. Of the basins with a combined hazard rankings of 4 in response to the 25-year storm, three (East Trout Creek [17], West Trout Creek [18], and Trout Creek tributary 1 [19]) are located in headwaters of Trout Creek, a tributary to the Rio Grande. Four others (44, 46, 47, and 48) are tributaries to the West Fork San Juan River. Leopard Creek (33) draining north out of the burned area and Hope Creek (41) draining east to a county road near U.S. Highway 160 also have combined hazard ranking of 4. Decker Creek (39) and Hope Creek (41), along with basin 40 (Lake Fork, combined hazard ranking of 3) could contribute debris flows which could impact U.S. Highway 160 on the eastern edge of the West Fork wildfire burn area (plate 3). Additionally, even small debris flows that affect structures and reservoirs at the basin outlets could cause damage.

Postwildfire Field Visit and Prewildfire Aerial Photography

A field visit to the area of the West Fork Fire Complex burn area on September 4, 2013, and inspection of prewildfire aerial photography indicated that debris flows, floods, or both, have produced debris-flow and alluvial fans in and adjacent to the burn area (figs. 2–19). Locations for each photograph in figures 2 through 19 are shown on figure 1. Whether these debris-flow or alluvial fans are caused or enhanced by increased runoff because of wildfires is unknown and beyond the scope of this report. However, the presence of these features throughout the area burned by the West Fork Fire Complex suggest that the region is at least minimally susceptible to potentially hazardous flooding or debris flows.

Caution may be necessary in or near the burn area during storms or high snowmelt regardless of the predicted debris-flow probability estimates in this report. The empirical models used in this report were constructed with variables important to debris-flow prediction only and are not designed to predict floods. Burn areas commonly produce floods during snowmelt and rainstorms that have hyper-concentrated sediment concentrations, which can be as damaging as debris flows, and may be more likely to travel to the mouth of large drainage basins than debris flows.

Areas where field reconnaissance was not possible were evaluated using prewildfire aerial photography and are shown in figures 2–5 and identified on figure 1. Figure 2 shows fan structures at the mouth of both Squaw and Little Squaw Creeks at the Rio Grande. Figure 3 shows a reach of upper Trout Creek and basin 19 and sediment erosion areas, which has an estimated debris-flow probability of 64 percent and debris-flow volume of 14,000 cubic meters in response to a 25-yr recurrence storm. Two fan structures, which may be alluvial or debris-flow deposits also are shown on figure 3. Figure 4 shows a reach of Goose Creek upstream from Lake Humphreys (plates 1–3) that contains erosion source areas for the fan deposits at the mouths of small tributary drainages. Figure 5 shows several fan deposits at the mouths of various watersheds between the mouths of Texas and Workman Creeks. Again, there is no direct evidence that wildfire was involved in the events that created these fan deposits.

One of the sites visited in the field was at Hope Creek (figs. 6–10), located about 3 miles east of U.S. Highway 160 where the forest road crosses Hope Creek. Figures 6–8 show evidence of debris-flow or alluvial deposits along Hope Creek including a fan structure and levees along the stream. Figure 9 shows erosion on a side-slope along Hope Creek that occurred in response to summer rains in 2013 after the West Fork Complex wildfire. Figure 10 shows the culvert at the forest road crossing Hope Creek. Culverts and bridges may become blocked during high streamflows and could back up water and cause failure of road embankments. The next drainage basin to the north is Lake Creek; figure 11 shows a debris-flow or alluvial fan cut by U.S. Highway 160 at the mouth at South Fork Rio Grande (fig. 1, plates 1–3).

Squaw Creek and Little Squaw Creek flow into the Rio Grande just downstream from Rio Grande Reservoir near Creede, Colorado. During a site visit to the mouth of Little Squaw Creek at the Rio Grande (fig. 1, plates 1–3), evidence of a large debris-flow or alluvial fan was identified (fig. 2). Unsorted deposits with large cobbles, boulders, and deformed trees on the surface of the fan are shown in figures 12–15 and small erosion channels were observed throughout the burned and unburned watershed in the study area. Figures 16 and 17 (location in fig. 1) provide examples of these channels along the Rio Grande downstream for a few miles below Rio Grande Reservoir (plates 1–3). The narrow channels with small drainage areas on steep slopes above the Rio Grande may be affected by avalanches, dry ravel, alluvial (water dominated) erosion, and debris-flow processes (fig. 16). The channels, while apparently active, do not contain large accumulations of debris or significant fans.

Goose Creek is a large basin that drains north to the Rio Grande near Wagon Wheel Gap and was partially burned in the West Fork Fire Complex (figs. 1 and 4, plates 1–3). The upper part of the drainage basin was burned, particularly the area upstream from Lake Humphreys (fig. 18), a reservoir formed by a large concrete arch dam with hydropower generation capacity (fig. 19). Figure 18 shows an alluvial fan at the Goose Creek inlet to Lake Humphreys (fig. 1). The burned slope in the background (top right) is basin 32 (debris-flow probability of 30 percent and debris-flow volume of 8,700 cubic meters in response to the 25-year storm), which could flow into the inlet area if triggered. Figure 19 is a photograph of the siphon for hydropower generation at Lake Humphreys that would likely be affected by floating debris flowing into the lake from upper Goose Creek.

Use and Limitations of the Maps

This assessment provides estimates of debris-flow probability and volume for drainage basins burned by the West Fork Fire Complex in response to three design storms based on predictive models developed from data from burned areas throughout the western United States. Larger, less-frequent storms are more likely to produce much larger debris flows. Because individual storms may not affect the entire area at any given time, debris flows may not be produced from all basins during storms. The estimates are most significant in the 3 years following the wildfire (Susan Cannon, U.S. Geological Survey, written commun., 2010).

Plates 1–3 may be used to prioritize areas where emergency-flood warnings or erosion mitigation may be needed prior to rainstorms within these basins, their outlets, or areas downstream from these basins. This assessment evaluates only potential postwildfire debris flows (Cannon and others, 2007). Substantial hazards from flash floods without debris flow may persist for many years after a fire.

This work is preliminary and is subject to revision and is being provided because of the need for timely "best science" information. The assessment is provided on the condition that neither the U.S. Geological Survey nor the United States Government may be held liable for any damages resulting from the authorized or unauthorized use of the assessment.

References Cited

Cannon, S.H., Gartner, J.E., and Michael, J.A., 2007, Methods for the emergency assessment of debris-flow hazards from basins burned by the fires of 2007, southern California: U.S. Geological Survey Open-File Report 2007–1384, 10 p. (Also available at *http://pubs.usgs.gov/of/2007/1384/*, accessed September 2013.)

Cannon, S.H., Gartner, J.E., Rupert, M.G., Michael, J.A., Rea, A.H., and Parrett, C., 2010, Predicting the probability and volume of postwildfire debris flows in the intermountain western United States: Geological Society of America Bulletin, v. 122, p. 127–144.

Cannon, S.H., Gartner, J.E., Wilson, R.C., and Laber, J.L., 2008, Storm rainfall conditions for floods and debris flows from recently burned areas in southwestern Colorado and southern California: Geomorphology, v. 96, p. 250–269, doi:10.1019/j.geomorph.2008.03.019.

Das, B.M., 1983, Advanced soil mechanics: New York, McGraw-Hill, 511 p.

ESRI, 2009, ArcGIS v. 9.3: Redlands, Calif., ESRI.

Gesch, D., Oimoen, M., Greenlee, S., Nelson, C., Steuck, M., and Tyler, D., 2002, The national elevation dataset: Photogrammetric Engineering and Remote Sensing, v. 68, no. 1, p. 5–11.

Helsel, D.R., and Hirsch, R.M., 2002, Statistical methods in water resources: New York, Elsevier Studies in Environmental Science, v. 49, 529 p.

Melton, M.A., 1965, The geomorphic and paleoclimate significance of alluvial deposits in southern Arizona: Journal of Geology, v. 73, p. 1–38.

National Soil Survey Center, 1991, State Soil Geographic (STATSGO) database—Data use information: U.S. Department of Agriculture, National Resources Conservation Service, Miscellaneous Publication 1492, 110 p. [Revised July, 1994]

Perica, S., Martin, D., Pavlovic, S., Roy, I., St. Laurent, M., Trypaluk, C., Unruh, D., Yekta, M., and Bannin, G., Precipitation-frequency atlas of the United States, Volume 8 Version 2.0: Midwestern states (Colorado, Iowa, Kansas, Michigan, Minnesota, Missouri, Nebraska, North Dakota, Oklahoma, South Dakota, Wisconsin): Silver Spring, Md., U.S. Department of Commerce, National Oceanic and Atmospheric Administration, National Weather Service, accessed September 2013, at *http://www.nws.noaa.gov/oh/hdsc/PF_documents/Atlas14_Volume8.pdf.*

Verdin, K.L., and Greenlee, S., 2003, Continuous parameterization using EDNA, in 2003 ESRI User's Conference, San Diego, Calif., July 7–11, 2003, Proceedings: Redlands, Calif., ESRI, accessed September 2013, at *http://gis.esri.com/library/userconf/proc03/p0617.pdf.*

Verdin, K.L., and Worstell, B., 2008, A fully distributed implementation of mean annual streamflow regional regression equations: Journal of the American Water Resources Association, v. 44, p. 1537–1547, doi: 10.1111/j.1752-1688.2008.00258.x

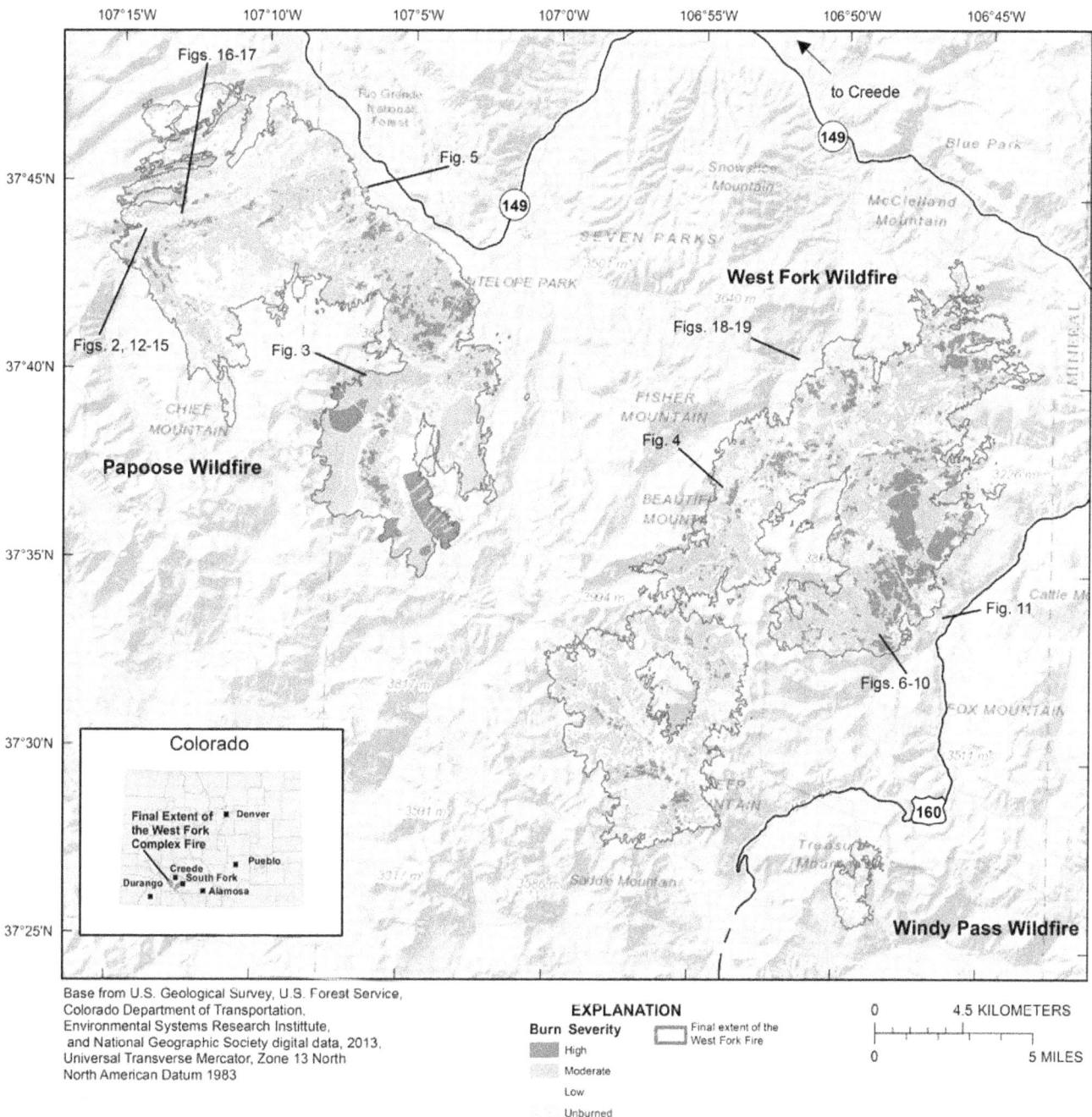

Figure 1. Location map with burn severity and locations of photographs in figures 2 through 19.

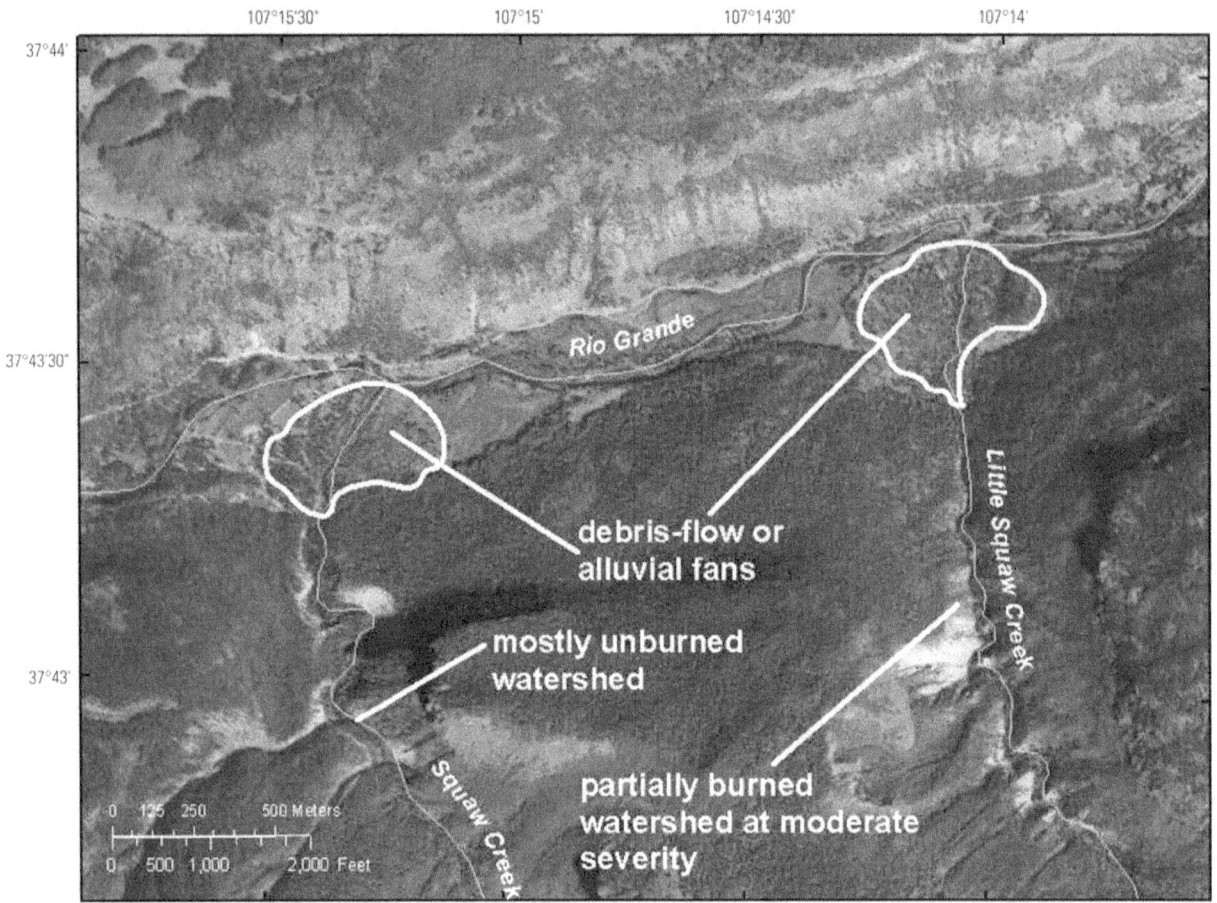

Figure 2. Aerial prewildfire photograph (NAIP Imagery, U.S. Department of Agriculture, Farm Service Agency, 2011) of lower reach of Little Squaw Creek and Squaw Creek (fig. 1) which flows from bottom to top of the image (south to north) into the Rio Grande west of Creede, Colo. Erosive areas are prominent in the lower part of the photograph, and a debris-flow fan is evident at the mouths of the watersheds at the Rio Grande.

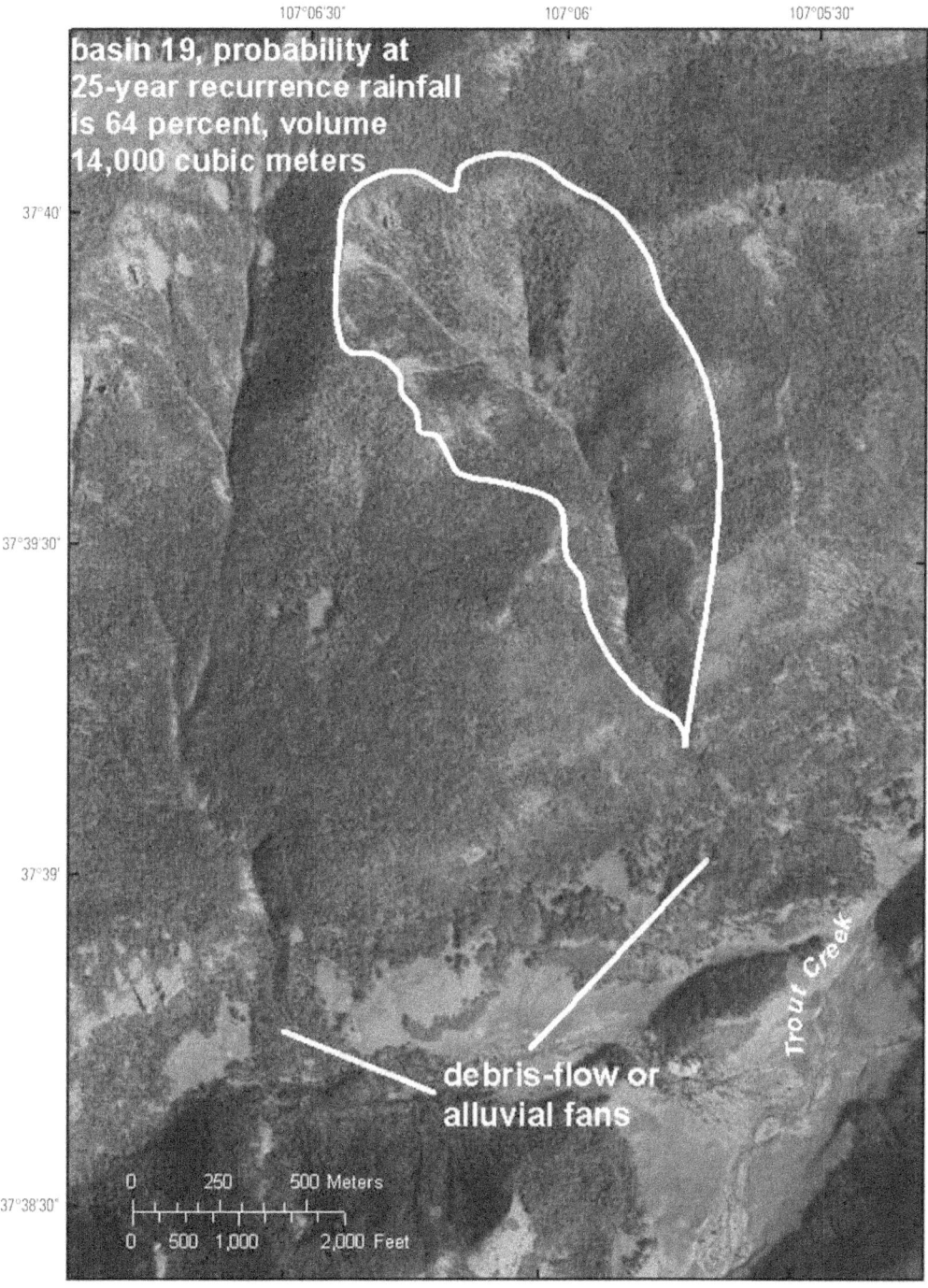

Figure 3. Aerial prewildfire photograph (NAIP Imagery, U.S. Department of Agriculture, Farm Service Agency, 2011) of upper Trout Creek (basin 19, fig. 1) which flows from bottom to top of the image (south to north) and then discharges into the Rio Grande west of Creede, Colo. Sediment erosion areas are prominent adjacent to beetle-killed spruce which burned in the West Fork Complex fire (Papoose burn).

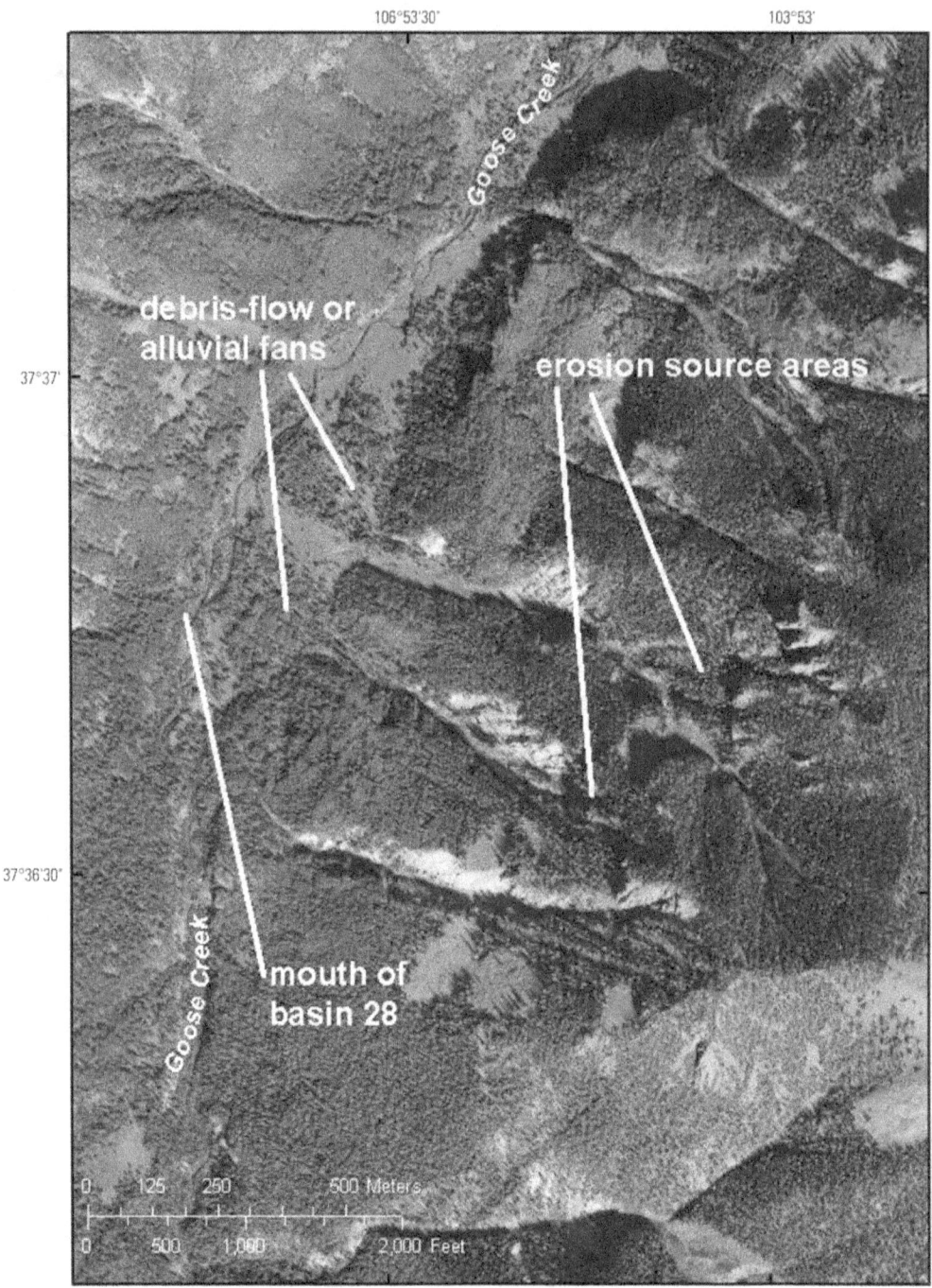

Figure 4. Aerial prewildfire photograph (NAIP Imagery, U.S. Department of Agriculture, Farm Service Agency, 2011) Goose Creek (fig. 1) which flows from bottom to top of the image (south to north) and eventually discharges into the Rio Grande east of Creede, Colo. Sediment erosion areas (located near basin 28 on plate 1) are prominent adjacent to beetle-killed spruce which burned in the West Fork Complex fire (West Fork burn).

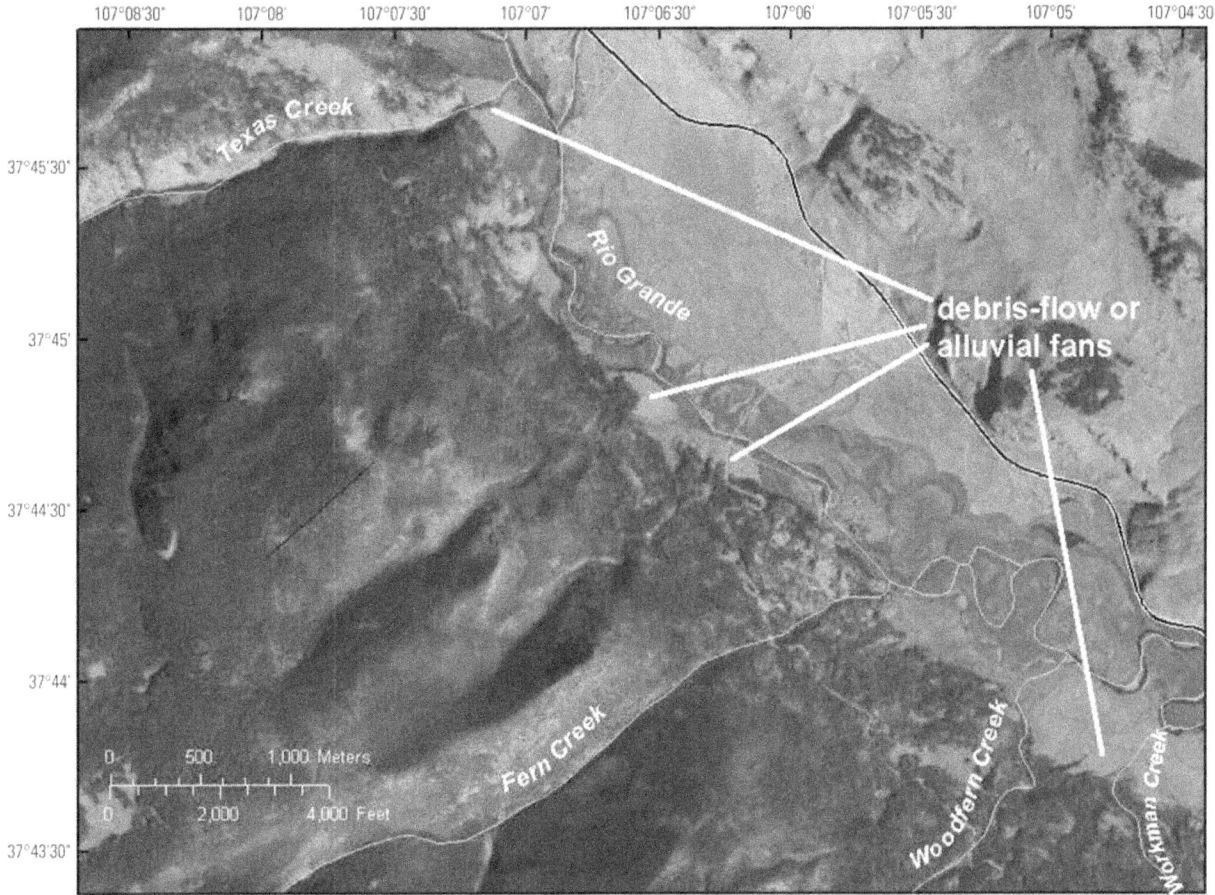

Figure 5. Aerial prewildfire photograph (NAIP Imagery, U.S. Department of Agriculture, Farm Service Agency, 2011) of area between the mouths of Texas Creek and Workman Creek along the Rio Grande (fig. 1). Fan structures of debris-flow, alluvial, or mixed origin are visible at the mouths of several creeks.

Figure 6.   Debris-flow or alluvial fan and levees in the Hope Creek watershed (basin 41), view upstream (fig. 1). (photograph by Michael Stevens)

Figure 7. Debris-flow or alluvial fan and debris-flow or alluvial levees in the Hope Creek watershed (basin 41) (fig. 1), taken a short distance upstream from figure 6. (photograph by Michael Stevens)

Figure 8.   Leading edge of debris-flow or alluvial fan eroded by Hope Creek (fig.1). (photograph by Michael Stevens)

Figure 9. Erosion of slope colluvium from late summer postfire rainfall in 2013 on slope adjacent to Hope Creek (fig.1). (photograph by Michael Stevens)

Figure 10.   Hope Creek (fig. 1) could transport debris that could obstruct the culvert at the forest road crossing and cause backup of water and possible failure of the road embankment. (photograph by Michael Stevens)

Figure 11. Road cut through debris-flow or alluvial fan deposit at the mouth of Lake Creek at U.S. Highway 160 (fig. 1). (photograph by Michael Stevens)

Figure 12. Little Squaw Creek (basin 4, plates 1-3) cutting through debris-flow or alluvial fan at the mouth at the Rio Grande (fig. 1). (photograph by Michael Stevens)

Figure 13. Relict dry channel through debris-flow or alluvial fan just east of active channel of Little Squaw Creek at the mouth at the Rio Grande (fig. 1). View downstream toward Rio Grande. (photograph by Michael Stevens)

Figure 14. Debris-flow or alluvial levee on fan feature at mouth of Little Squaw Creek at the Rio Grande (fig. 1) (Note rock resting on tree trunk). (photograph by Michael Stevens)

Figure 15. Trees possibly deformed by debris-flow or alluvial material on Little Squaw Creek fan at the Rio Grande (fig. 1). (photograph by Michael Stevens)

Figure 16. Narrow channels (fig. 1) with small drainage areas on steep slopes above the Rio Grande (flows right to left) that may be affected by avalanche, dry ravel, alluvial (water dominated) erosion, and debris-flow processes. (photograph by Michael Stevens)

Figure 17. Erosion channels at base of steep slope at Rio Grande downstream from Little Squaw Creek (fig. 1), while apparently active, do not have large accumulations of debris or significant fans, possibly indicating relatively small potential debris-flow volumes. (photograph by Michael Stevens)

Figure 18. Alluvial fan at inlet to Lake Humphreys on Goose Creek (fig. 1). Burned slope in the background (top right) is basin 32 (probability of 30 percent and volume of 8,700 cubic meters with the 25-year recurrence 1-hour rainfall) which could flow into the inlet area if triggered. (photograph by Michael Stevens)

Figure 19. Siphon for hydropower generation at Lake Humphreys (fig. 1) could be affected by floating debris flowing into the lake from upper Goose Creek. (photograph by Michael Stevens)

Table 1. Estimated debris-flow probabilities, volumes, and combined hazard rankings for the 2013 West Fork Fire Complex in southwestern Colorado.

[dd, decimal degrees; mm, millimeters; km², square kilometers; %, percent; m³, cubic meters; <, less than; >, greater than]

Basin identifier	Description	Basin Pour Point Latitude (dd)	Basin Pour Point Longitude (dd)	Drainage area (km²)	Area burned at moderate or high severity (km²)	2-year/1-hour precipitation 14–24 mm (average 19 mm) Probability (%)	Volume (m³)	Combined hazard ranking	10-year/1-hour precipitation 21–34 mm (average 29 mm) Probability (%)	Volume (m³)	Combined hazard ranking	25-year/1-hour precipitation 27–45 mm (average 35 mm) Probability (%)	Volume (m³)	Combined hazard ranking
1	House Canyon	37.7889	−107.1832	10.7	2.4	1	30,000	2	2	38,000	2	3	43,000	2
2	Road Canyon	37.7874	−107.1732	25.3	3.9	1	73,000	3	1	91,000	3	2	>100,000	3
3	Ingalls Gulch	37.7794	−107.1477	2.7	0.8	1	10,000	2	3	13,000	2	4	15,000	2
4	Little Squaw Creek	37.6879	−107.2007	30.0	2.4	<1	67,000	3	1	85,000	3	1	98,000	3
5	Rio Grande tributary 1	37.7299	−107.2266	0.9	0.7	4	3,100	1	7	3,900	1	12	4,500	1
6	Papoose Creek	37.7362	−107.1940	8.3	3.7	2	33,000	2	4	42,000	2	7	48,000	2
7	Rio Grande tributary 2	37.7374	−107.1872	1.3	1.1	14	6,600	2	27	8,500	2	39	9,800	3
8	Texas Creek	37.7444	−107.1560	30.0	6.3	<1	73,000	3	1	94,000	3	1	>100,000	3
9	Texas Creek tributary	37.7558	−107.1437	1.9	1.0	2	5,800	2	3	7,400	2	6	8,500	2
10	Rio Grande tributary 3	37.7553	−107.1182	1.3	1.1	9	5,600	2	19	7,200	2	28	8,300	2
11	Rio Grande tributary 4	37.7460	−107.1124	1.6	1.1	7	7,400	2	14	9,500	2	22	11,000	2
12	Rio Grande tributary 5	37.7409	−107.1079	1.1	0.7	7	6,100	2	14	7,800	2	22	8,900	2
13	Fern Creek	37.7384	−107.0892	8.4	5.7	9	51,000	3	18	66,000	3	27	75,000	3
14	Woodfern Creek	37.7354	−107.0813	10.1	5.1	4	62,000	3	9	79,000	3	15	90,000	3
15	Workman Creek	37.7284	−107.0756	4.7	4.3	15	22,000	2	27	28,000	3	38	32,000	3
16	Cliff Creek	37.7071	−107.0500	5.0	5.0	19	20,000	2	32	25,000	3	43	28,000	3
17	East Trout Creek	37.6360	−107.0938	29.5	13.2	8	>100,000	3	14	>100,000	3	21	>100,000	4
18	West Trout Creek	37.6448	−107.0914	28.3	13.2	6	>100,000	3	14	>100,000	3	21	>100,000	4
19	Trout Creek tributary 1	37.6498	−107.0889	1.3	1.2	34	9,700	3	52	12,000	3	64	14,000	4
20	Copper Creek	37.6582	−107.0804	7.7	1.9	1	23,000	2	1	29,000	2	2	32,000	2
21	Trout Creek tributary 2	37.6654	−107.0712	0.3	0.3	35	2,400	2	52	2,900	3	63	3,300	3
22	Trout Creek tributary 3	37.6655	−107.0711	1.2	0.4	1	5,400	2	1	6,700	2	2	7,500	2
23	Jumper Creek	37.6720	−107.0602	8.4	3.0	2	37,000	2	4	47,000	2	6	54,000	3
24	Trout Creek tributary 4	37.6789	−107.0347	3.3	2.0	2	8,300	2	4	10,000	2	6	11,000	2

Table 1. Estimated debris-flow probabilities, volumes, and combined hazard rankings for the 2013 West Fork Fire Complex in southwestern Colorado.—Continued

[dd, decimal degrees; mm, millimeters; km², square kilometers; %, percent, m³, cubic meters; <, less than; >, greater than]

Basin identifier	Description	Basin Pour Point				2-year/1-hour precipitation 14–24 mm (average 19 mm)			10-year/1-hour precipitation 21–34 mm (average 29 mm)			25-year/1-hour precipitation 27–45 mm (average 35 mm)		
		Latitude (dd)	Longitude (dd)	Drainage area (km²)	Area burned at moderate or high severity (km²)	Probability (%)	Volume (m³)	Combined hazard ranking	Probability (%)	Volume (m³)	Combined hazard ranking	Probability (%)	Volume (m³)	Combined hazard ranking
25	Middle Creek	37.6485	–107.0358	11.1	5.3	2	40,000	2	3	48,000	2	5	53,000	3
26	Goose Creek 1	37.6016	–106.8959	29.6	9.0	3	>100,000	3	5	>100,000	3	8	>100,000	3
27	Goose Creek tributary 1	37.6050	–106.8961	4.0	0.5	<1	12,000	2	1	15,000	2	1	16,000	2
28	Goose Creek tributary 2	37.6124	–106.8963	1.4	0.2	<1	6,000	2	1	7,200	2	1	8,100	2
29	Goose Creek tributary 3	37.6197	–106.8901	1.6	0.4	1	7,700	2	2	9,200	2	3	10,000	2
30	Goose Creek tributary 4	37.6312	–106.8780	6.9	1.5	1	23,000	2	1	27,000	2	2	31,000	2
31	Goose Creek tributary 5	37.6387	–106.8731	2.5	1.7	5	11,000	2	9	13,000	2	14	14,000	2
32	Goose Creek tributary 6	37.6686	–106.8569	1.3	1.0	15	6,600	2	23	7,800	2	30	8,700	3
33	Leopard Creek	37.6782	–106.8232	23.7	15.0	6	>100,000	3	11	>100,000	3	16	>100,000	4
34	Leopard Creek tributary	37.6817	–106.8000	2.7	2.3	19	14,000	2	31	17,000	3	43	19,000	3
35	Elk Creek	37.6952	–106.7408	10.4	4.7	3	53,000	3	5	64,000	3	8	72,000	3
36	Raspberry Gulch	37.6804	–106.7401	6.1	4.3	5	23,000	2	10	28,000	2	15	32,000	3
37	Trout Creek (south) tributary	37.6395	–106.7519	12.1	5.2	2	46,000	2	3	56,000	3	5	63,000	3
38	Trout Creek (south)	37.6311	–106.7620	6.2	4.6	7	24,000	2	14	29,000	2	20	32,000	3
39	Decker Creek	37.6131	–106.7608	10.7	9.1	21	84,000	3	34	>100,000	4	45	>100,000	5
40	Lake Fork	37.5626	–106.7687	28.5	14.0	3	>100,000	3	6	>100,000	3	10	>100,000	3
41	Hope Creek	37.5473	–106.7876	27.6	15.0	14	>100,000	3	24	>100,000	4	34	>100,000	4
42	Cimarron Creek	37.5144	–106.9578	29.5	6.2	3	>100,000	3	7	>100,000	3	10	>100,000	3
43	Cimarron Creek tributary	37.5142	–106.9579	5.0	1.3	4	23,000	2	8	27,000	2	12	30,000	2
44	West Fork San Juan River 1	37.5129	–106.9550	15.0	3.8	10	81,000	3	18	98,000	3	25	>100,000	4
45	West Fork San Juan River tributary 1	37.5082	–106.9467	1.3	0.1	3	5,800	2	6	7,000	2	8	7,700	2

Table 1. Estimated debris-flow probabilities, volumes, and combined hazard rankings for the 2013 West Fork Fire Complex in southwestern Colorado.—Continued

[dd, decimal degrees; mm, millimeters; km², square kilometers; %, percent, m³, cubic meters; <, less than; >, greater than]

| Basin identifier | Description | Basin Pour Point | | Drainage area (km²) | Area burned at moderate or high severity (km²) | 2-year/1-hour precipitation 14–24 mm (average 19 mm) | | | 10-year/1-hour precipitation 21–34 mm (average 29 mm) | | | 25-year/1-hour precipitation 27–45 mm (average 35 mm) | | |
		Latitude (dd)	Longitude (dd)			Probability (%)	Volume (m³)	Combined hazard ranking	Probability (%)	Volume (m³)	Combined hazard ranking	Probability (%)	Volume (m³)	Combined hazard ranking
46	West Fork San Juan River tributary 2	37.4950	−106.9352	1.2	0.9	65	9,100	4	77	11,000	4	83	12,000	4
47	West Fork San Juan River tributary 3	37.4932	−106.9354	1.9	1.1	40	12,000	3	55	15,000	3	65	16,000	4
48	Beaver Creek	37.5244	−106.9118	30.0	9.4	6	>100,000	3	11	>100,000	3	17	>100,000	4
49	Beaver Creek tributary	37.5118	−106.9233	2.7	0.7	4	13,000	2	7	15,000	2	10	17,000	2
50	West Fork San Juan River tributary 4	37.4867	−106.9303	2.1	0.3	2	8,500	2	4	10,000	2	5	11,000	2
51	West Fork San Juan River tributary 5	37.4849	−106.9302	3.1	0.7	5	15,000	2	9	18,000	2	13	20,000	2
52	Burro Creek	37.4724	−106.9272	7.0	1.0	1	24,000	2	2	29,000	2	3	32,000	2
53	West Fork San Juan River tributary 6	37.4719	−106.9263	1.2	0.6	19	8,300	2	30	9,900	2	38	11,000	3
54	Treasure Creek	37.4265	−106.8227	3.2	0.5	1	12,000	2	2	15,000	2	3	16,000	2